# Mother Murphy's Law

## by Bruce Lansky

## Illustrations by Christine Tripp

Meadowbrook

Distributed by Simon and Schuster
New York

# Acknowledgements

I want to thank the following people for their help in creating a number of the laws that appear in this book:

Donna Ahrens
Mitch Lansky
Ramona Mueller

Carol Garzona
Bonnie St. James
Shelley Tromberg

I also want to gratefully acknowledge the help, encouragement and feedback I received from the following people:

Susan and Eric Brundlie
K. C. Stabeck
Joan Spence
Marge Hughes
Heidi Meyers
Sue Veazie
Barb Stigall

Pam Pierre
Sarah Barker
Penny Warner
Chris Larsen
Barb DeGroot
Pat Onken
Pat O'Neil

Without them this book would not have been the same.

Published by Meadowbrook, Inc., Deephaven, MN

BOOK TRADE DISTRIBUTION by Simon & Schuster, a division of Simon & Schuster, Inc., 1230 Avenue of the Americas, New York, NY 10020

ISBN 0-88166-080-9

**S&S Ordering #: 0-671-62274-9 Priced**

89 90 10 9 8 7 6 5 4 3

Printed in the United States of America

Author: Bruce Lansky
Editor: Christine Larsen
Photography: Peter Poon On Wong
Illustrations: Christine Tripp
Design: Nancy MacLean
Keyline: Mike Tuminelly
Production: John Howard

# Table of Contents

# Introduction

Your own mother wouldn't tell you. (She didn't want to rain on your parade.) Dr. Spock, T. Berry Brazelton, Elisabeth Bing and Penelope Leach didn't write it in their books. (It doesn't sound professional.) Erma Bombeck and Theresa Bloomingdale wrote about it. (But they're primarily storytellers who didn't express their insights in the form of laws.) Murphy himself was too busy testing airplanes to notice it.

Mother Murphy is the only one who comes right out and says it. She's got no reason to mince words. She's got no professional reputation to protect or syndicated column to promote. (What the heck, she's not even real!)

Mother Murphy had to learn about motherhood the hard way. Just like every other mother before her. It wasn't until her son, a development engineer testing airplanes for the Air Force, enunciated his now-famous law that she realized it explained a lot more than why airplanes crash, computers break down and American business continues to search for excellence. It was Mother Murphy's genius to apply "Murphy's Law" to family life.

She knows that your baby will cry the moment you finally nod off to sleep and wet his diaper the moment you've changed him into a clean one. And she knows that your toddler will stumble into your bedroom as soon as you start making love.

She's not afraid to tell the truth about what little girls are really made of. And she's got plenty of helpful advice. Like a surefire method to conceive, and a sure cure for colic. She'll tell you what vegetables your

1

child *will* eat and how to figure out which child really started the fight, without tearing out anyone's fingernails. She can even tell you how to open up channels of communication with your entire family, when you think there's no way.

Mother Murphy gives you the kind of advice about having babies and being a parent that you won't find anywhere else. If Mother Murphy didn't exist, someone would have to invent her. So I did.

Why, you ask, did a man write *Mother Murphy's Law*? Good question. I'm a single parent with joint custody. When my children are with me, I have to play both the father's and mother's roles. I cook, clean, comfort, coach and handle complaints. This dual role isn't new for me. When my children were younger, their mother traveled around the country promoting her child care books while I stayed home to take care of the children. That was before "Mr. Mom" made child care a popular pastime for dads.

So maybe it takes a klutzy dad to make sense out of parenting.

Before I discovered "Mother Murphy's Law," I was very, very frustrated. Nothing I did seemed to work. My cooking wasn't as good as Mom's. I wasn't as sensitive or as sympathetic as Mom. Even my jokes produced groans. But now that I know in advance that whatever I do won't work, I don't feel so inadequate. I don't worry as much. I don't feel so guilty. In fact, I enjoy being a parent a lot more.

Don't get me wrong. Having children is one of life's most rewarding experiences. Particularly if you're into delayed gratification. I no longer fall apart when my kids are destroying each other or my house. I'm not surprised. I just smile and say to myself: "Mother Murphy was right." And when my children bring home a good report card or help me with the dishes, I'm a very happy father (or mother, depending on how you look at it).

Like you, I want the best for my children. "Mother Murphy's Law" makes it a lot easier to accept whatever happens and love my children as they really are.

# Mother Murphy's Law

1. Everything your parents did was wrong.
2. Now that you're a parent, everything you do is wrong.
3. Your children will take credit for anything that happens to go right.

### Corollary

The harder you try not to, the more likely you are to repeat your parents' mistakes.

# Mother Murphy's Best Advice

1. Hope for the best.
2. Prepare for the worst.
3. Love them no matter what.

### Corollary

The higher your expectations, the more disappointed you'll be.

# Mother Murphy's Discovery

Mothers know best...but no one ever listens.

# Parenthood

## The Tender Trap

Parenthood is much easier to get into than out of.

## The Basket Case

If your spouse hasn't already driven you nuts, your kids will.

## Theresa Bloomingdale's Discovery

Murphy must have been a mother.

4

## Parents' Job Description

1. Parenting is a 24-hour-a-day job with no salary, no raises, no promotions and very few vacations.

2. Parents are responsible for everything that happens to their children.

3. Guilt and self-blame are occupational hazards.

4. Parents don't get workers' compensation or any other fringe benefits.

5. Parents can never retire—even when their kids ask them to.

6. Parents "don't get no respect"—until they die—and then it's too late.

## The First Law of Parenthood

Nobody really wants your job, but everybody thinks they can do it better.

## The Second Law of Parenthood

Those who think they can do it better messed up when they had the chance.

## The Doctrine of Awesome Responsibility

The more you consider the awesome fact that you are completely responsible for a human life, the more you miss the point that no matter what you say or do, your child will pay little or no attention and blithely do whatever she wants, anyway.

### The Law of Good and Bad Genes

1. Bad traits are inherited from your spouse's side of the family.

2. Good traits are inherited from your side of the family.

### The Parenting Lesson

1. By the time you've finally learned something about raising children, you're a grandparent.

2. What you've learned is how little you know about the subject.

### The Limits of Your Endurance

1. You don't know what the limits of your endurance are until you've had children.

2. From infancy on, your children will discover those limits and push you beyond them.

### The Law of Parental Advice

No matter what advice you give your children, they will ignore 80 percent and misinterpret the rest.


# Grandparents

### The Grandparents' Vindication

You can never appreciate your parents' hard work and sacrifice until you have children of your own. That's why your parents are so happy when you have children.

## The Law of Grandmotherly Omniscience

Your mother knows best. About everything. And she'll never let you forget it.

### Corollary

You didn't listen when you were young. And you still don't.

## The Relaxation Response

1. Your parents will be a lot less uptight with your children than they were with you.

2. You would be, too, if you only saw your children once or twice a month and could send them home when they misbehaved.

## The "Spoil" Sport

The stricter you are with your children, the harder your parents work at spoiling them.

# Working Mothers

## Nomenclature Nonsense

Why do they call mothers who work "working mothers"? They don't call fathers who work "working fathers"!

## The Supermom Alternative

You don't have to be a Supermom to succeed in both your career and child-rearing. All you need is a $75,000 job and live-in help.

## The Tuition Toll

The day after you get a raise at work, your day-care center will inform you that tuition is being increased.

### Addendum

The increase in tuition will exceed your raise.

## The Supermom Syndrome

You can always pick out the Supermom at a business lunch. She's the one who reaches for her American Express card and pulls out a pacifier instead.

# Experts

## The Expert Enigma

When you consult an expert, you get five problems:

1. The original problem.

2. Understanding the advice.

3. Implementing the advice.

4. The new problem that resulted from implementing the advice.

5. The staggering bill.

### Addendum

The more experts you consult, the more solutions you'll find for any parenting problem.

## The Law of Expertology

The solution to any parenting problem depends on which expert you ask.

## The Curse of Expertise

Why is it that the children of most psychologists you know are weird?

Why is it that the children of most ministers and rabbis you know are delinquents?

## The Power of the Printed Word

The effectiveness of your favorite discipline book is enhanced when you wave it menacingly in the air as you chase your caught-in-the-act child into his bedroom.

### Corollary

Psychologists know best. About writing books.

# Stages

## The Dissatisfaction Doctrine

1.  Babies can never be held enough.

2.  Children can never get enough attention.

3.  Teenagers can never get enough space.

4.  Parents can never get enough time for themselves.

## The Inevitability of Advice

1. When you're pregnant, everyone gives you advice.

2. After you've had your baby, everyone gives you advice.

3. When your baby becomes a teenager, everyone gives you advice—especially your teenager.

4. When your teenager "leaves the nest," everyone gives you advice.

5. When you become a grandparent, you get to pass on all that good advice to your children.

## The Curious Convolution

1. At three, he asks, "Why?"

2. At seven, he asks, "Why not?"

3. At twelve, he asks, "Are you kidding?"

4. At thirteen, he says, "Cut the crap!"

5. After that, it's all downhill.

## The Transportation Tangle

1. The baby in the carriage will want to climb out.

2. The baby in the backpack will want to walk.

3. The child on foot will want to be carried.

4. The child on the trike will want to ride a two-wheeler.

5. The teenager on the ten-speed bike will want your car.

6. The teenager with your car will want a sports car.

# The Hiding Hassle

1. No matter where you hide the cookies, your kids will find them.

2. No matter where you hide your Playboy magazines, your teenagers will find them.

### Corollary

No matter where you hide your liquor, your cleaning woman will find it.

## The Negative Nuisance

1. Your toddler says, "No."

2. Your schoolchild says, "No way, José."

3. Your pre-teen says, "Forget it."

4. Your teenager no longer speaks your language.

## The Theory of Relativity as Applied to Humor

1. Your baby laughs only when you tickle her.
2. Your toddler laughs at all of your jokes.
3. Your schoolchild laughs at some of your jokes.
4. Your teenager groans at all of your jokes.
5. You laugh when you hear your grown daughter telling the same jokes to her child.

## Thanks, but No Thanks

1. Babies are incapable of saying "thank you."
2. Children forget.
3. Teenagers are incapable of appreciating anything you do.

# Prenatal

## Pre- and Postnatal Advice

Before you have a baby your family says:

1. "You'd make such great parents."
2. "You don't know what you're missing."
3. "Children add a whole new dimension to your marriage."
4. "Besides, you need heirs to carry on the family line."

After your baby is born, they say, "Here comes trouble!"

## The Population Solution

If men had babies, there'd be no population problem.

# Conception

## Sure-Fire Conception Plan

1. Tell your parents that you've decided not to have children.

2. Go deeply into debt.

3. Move into an expensive one-bedroom apartment with a three-year lease.

4. Buy a two-door sports coupe.

5. Finally lose ten pounds and fit perfectly into all your clothes.

6. File for adoption.

## Four Reasons for Becoming Pregnant

1. You'll finally have cleavage.

2. Your complexion will clear up.

3. You can have sex without worrying about getting pregnant.

4. You'll be able to get a seat on a bus or train. (Unless you live in New York.)

## The Ironclad Law of Genetic Determination

If your parents were unable to have children, you won't be able to have children either.

## The Sexual Sacrifice

1. The harder you try to conceive, the less you enjoy sex.

2. The more children you've had, the less time you have for sex.

## Sure-Fire Advance Method for Sex Determination

1. If most of the baby shower gifts you receive are blue, your baby will be a girl.

2. If most of the baby shower gifts you receive are pink, your baby will be a boy.

3. If most of the baby shower gifts you receive are lavender, your friends are gay.

## The Financial Factor

By the time you can afford to start a family, you're too old to do it. (And you know enough not to.)

# Pregnancy

## The Weight Gain Question

1. The woman in your childbirth preparation class who asks all the other pregnant women how much weight they've gained is the only one whose weight gain has been textbook perfect.

2. At the six-week postpartum reunion, she's the one who fits into her size-three jeans while everyone else is still wearing maternity pants.

# The Announcement Annoyance

The sooner you announce your pregnancy, the more often you'll hear people say:

1. "Are you *still* pregnant?!"

2. "Seems like you've been pregnant forever!"

3. "You must be trying to set a new record for gestation."

4. "Gee, I didn't know you were expecting again. . . . Oh, you mean this is still the same pregnancy?"

## Helpful Hint

Don't announce your pregnancy until you hear snickers every time you turn sideways.


# The Gestation Duration

An elephant's gestational period is two years.
In humans, it only seems that long.


# The Overdue Predicament

How to tell when you're overdue:

1. All your childbirth classmates have already had their babies.

2. You can't remember what it was like not being pregnant.

3. You get twenty phone calls a day from friends and relatives, all of whom are "just wondering how you are."

4. You burst into tears whenever the phone rings.

## Waistline Wisdom for Women

Take a photo of your waistline as soon as you're sure you've conceived. You may never see it again.

## The Mystery of Birth

No matter how hard you try, you can't imagine how your eight-pound, twenty-inch baby will ever squeeze out.

## How To Make the Most of Your Belly

1.  Use it as a book rest.

2.  Use it as a TV table.

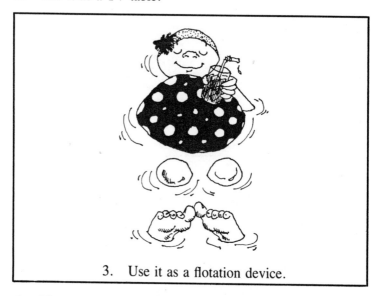

3.  Use it as a flotation device.

4.  Use it as part of a Santa Claus costume.

5.  Use it as an excuse.

6.  Rent it out for billboard advertising.

## Prenatal Hide 'n Seek

1.  The moment your husband puts his hand on your belly, your baby will stop moving.

2.  The moment he removes his hand, your baby will give a monumental kick.

## The Calendar Distortion

The ninth month is the longest month.

### Reassurance

You can't be pregnant forever.

### Corollary

Sooner or later, "something's got to give." Just hope it's not your sanity.

## The Long-Overdue Predicament

How to tell when you're long overdue:

Your obstetrician has retired. His son has taken over his practice.

# Labor

## The Childbirth Instructor's Secret Code

When your childbirth instructor says "contraction," what she's really talking about is "pain."

## Mother Murphy's Law of Labor

The more advanced your labor, the greater the odds that:

1. Your car won't start.
2. There's new construction on the fastest route to the hospital.
3. You make a wrong turn and get lost.
4. You arrive at a railroad crossing just in time to watch a long freight train going past at two miles per hour.
5. You can't find a parking space in the hospital lot.
6. There is no attendant on duty at the hospital admissions desk.
7. You don't have the proper health insurance information with you.
8. Your obstetrician is playing golf and can't be reached.

### Corollary

The more advanced your labor, the longer and more complicated the hospital admission forms.

## The Calmness Contradiction

No matter how regular and strong her contractions are, the mother-to-be will be calmer than her driver. Until she reaches the hospital.

# The Childbirth Clue

If having a baby were easy, they wouldn't take you to the "labor room." They'd take you to the "party room."

## The Pain Predicament

1.  The more it hurts, the less likely you are to remember any of the breathing exercises that were supposed to take your mind off the pain.

2.  The more it hurts, the more likely you are to beg for every drug they told you not to take in your childbirth preparation class. Plus some they didn't even mention.

## The Inspection Syndrome

The number of people who check your dilation during labor is equal to the number of people passing by your labor room door.

## The Amnesia Effect

Childbirth produces amnesia: The more painful the experience, the more joyfully you recall it.

# Babies

## The Teething Tenet

If a baby had a tooth for every time his parents said, "He's so fussy, he must be cutting a tooth," he'd be a crocodile.

## The Helping Hassle

There are three reasons for not accepting your mother-in-law's offer to help you with your new baby. You'll have:

1. One more mouth to feed.

2. One more person to clean up after.

3. More unwanted advice than you can possibly use in a lifetime.

## The Test of Time

Grandmothers who coo at infants and get all misty-eyed have forgotten what baby care was really like.

## The Emergency Expectation

Emergencies only occur when:

1. You are alone with the baby.

2. All the stores are closed.

3. There's a blizzard raging outside.

4. Your car won't start.

5. You can't get through to your doctor.

6. It's the Friday night preceding a three-day holiday weekend.

# In the Hospital

## First Words After Giving Birth

1. English mothers say, "Blimey!"

2. Irish mothers say, "Faith and begorra!"

3. Italian mothers say, "Mama Mia!"

4. German mothers say, "Ach du lieber!"

5. French mothers say, "Sacre Bleu!"

6. Jewish mothers say, "Oy Gevalt!"

7. Norwegian mothers say, "Oof-da!"

8. Spanish mothers say, "Ay Caramba!"

Roughly translated, these expressions all have about the same meaning: "What have I gotten myself into?"

## The Resemblance Riddle

Your newborn will resemble Mr. Magoo. Mr. Magoo will deny paternity.

## The Aural Ambiguity

All newborn babies sound alike. But yours is louder.

## How To Recognize Your Baby

The one infant in the hospital nursery who is *not* asleep and is bawling, waving her arms wildly in the air and kicking her covers off is yours.

## The Pain Principle

A new mother who has just gone through a long and painful labor and delivery will weep when her newborn has to have his heel pricked by the nurse.

### "Says Who?"

After you survive a long and painful delivery, your husband will describe the experience as "a piece of cake."

### Visiting Rules

1. As soon as you have taken your baby back to the nursery and settled down for a much-needed nap, ten visitors will show up.

2. Your "perfect angel" will start to fuss the minute your visitors arrive.

### Excerpts from the Baby Owner's Manual

1. Babies leak. From both ends.

2. Babies do not meet the latest EPA emission control standards.

3. Babies do not meet the latest EPA noise control standards, either.

4. Babies cost more than $200,000 to feed, clothe and educate.

5. Babies come with no guarantees.

6. Babies have no trade-in value.

# Crying and Sleep

### The Roller Coaster Riddle

What gets you down in the daytime and keeps you up at night? (Hint: You can't buy it at the drugstore.)

## The Crying Baby Options

1.  Comfort the baby every time he cries and risk reinforcing the crying behavior, thus increasing its frequency.
    Result: Both parents will get little or no sleep at night.

2.  Let the baby cry in the hope that after awhile he will become totally exhausted and fall asleep naturally.
    Result: Both parents will get little or no sleep at night.

## Occupational Obstacles

1.  When you're not changing your baby, she's wet.

2.  When you're not feeding your baby, she's hungry.

3.  When you're not holding your baby, she's fussy.

4.  When you're not changing, feeding or holding your baby, she's crying.

### Corollary

Taking care of your baby is easy, as long as you don't have anything else to do.

## The Relationship Riddle

1.  If the baby never cries or fusses and sleeps through the night, it's your neighbor's.

2.  If the baby cries and fusses all day and night, it's yours.

3.  If the baby is an "angel," you're its grandmother.

4.  If the baby is a "pain in the butt," you're the older sibling.

## Parenting Proficiency

Just because your baby is crying doesn't mean you're a lousy parent. Just a guilty one.

## The Siumber Secrets

1. The moment your fussing baby finally falls asleep in your arms, the phone will ring.

2. The moment you put your baby in her crib, she'll wake up.

## The Sleep Solution

Rhythmic background noises help lull babies to sleep. Bring your baby into your bed and put her beside your snoring spouse and she will go right to sleep. Unfortunately, the snoring keeps *you* awake.

## The Family Bed Phobia

Making love while your baby is sleeping in your bedroom is like dancing to ''Whole Lotta Shakin' Goin' On'' on tiptoes.

## The Family Bed Blues

The smaller the baby, the more space in your bed he will occupy.

## The $64,000 Question

When your baby finally begins sleeping through the night, will you still remember how to make love?

# Doctors

## The Ultimate Colic Solution

Book a first-class cabin for two on a slow boat to China for your baby and a deaf wet nurse.

## The Spock Syndrome

1. The solutions to all your baby's problems are in Dr. Spock's book.

2. By the time you get the book off the shelf and find the right page, you've got two new problems to look up.

## The Colic Prognosis

1. When babies cry interminably for no apparent reason, they have "colic."

2. When your baby has colic, *you* may cry interminably for no apparent reason. You don't have colic. You are exhausted and depressed.

# The Waiting Game

1. The fussier your baby, the longer you'll have to wait in the waiting room before being seen.

2. The longer you wait in the waiting room, the longer you'll have to wait in the examination room.

3. The longer you wait in the examination room, the less time the doctor will have to spend with you.

# The Limits of Medical Knowledge

There is no known cure for either colic or the common cold.
Result: You have a cold you can't shake, from staying up nights listening to your colicky baby.

# The Pediatric Prescription

No matter how sick you think your baby is when you call your pediatrician, you'll be told: "Don't worry. Your baby's condition is perfectly normal."

# The Medicine Malady

The more important it is to get all the medication into your baby's tummy, the greater the probability it will end up all over your baby or you.

### Corollaries

1. When baby's medicine is clear, it never spills.

2. When the medicine is bright red, it spills all over baby, you, and the furniture.

# Diapers

## What Little Boys and Girls Are Really Made Of

When you first change your baby's diapers you discover:

1.  Your son *is* made of "snips and snails and puppy dogs' tails." Plus a few other things Mother Goose neglected to mention.

2.  So is your daughter.

## The Law of Leaks

Leakproof diapers aren't.

## The Dirty Diaper Dilemma

The sooner you check your baby's diaper, the sooner you'll find that it is wet.

### Addendum

The more often you change your son's diaper, the more often *you'll* get wet.

# Daddies

## Daddy's Law

Fathers greet "unusual smells" from babies with the remark, "I think you need to see Mommy now."

## The Paternal Escape Clause

Dads don't like to be awakened in the middle of the night. After all, they have to go "to work" the next day.

## The "Daddy's Home" Dilemma

After you've spent all afternoon rocking and singing baby to sleep, Daddy will come home and wake her for a "gymnastic workout."

## 2 a.m. Sound Effects

1. You can hear your baby's cries even though the door is closed, there's a pillow over your head, and you're wearing ear plugs.

2. Fathers with perfectly normal hearing can't hear a thing.

# Dressing

## An Ounce of Prevention

Whenever you wear nursing pads, you won't need them. The one time you go out in public without pads, your blouse will get soaked through.

## The Dressing Dilemma

1. The more expensive the baby outfit, the more difficult it is to put on.

2. The longer it takes to put on, the sooner baby will spit up.

3. The amount a baby spits up is in direct proportion to how dressed up the baby and you are.

### Corollary

The more expensive the outfit, the sooner baby will outgrow it.

## Shutter-Bugs

1. When your baby is all dressed up and looking picture-perfect, you won't have any film in your camera.

2. When you aim a camera at your smiling baby, your baby will start to cry.

## The Attraction Axiom

A clean business suit attracts baby burps and cat hairs.

# Eating

## The Bottle Is Greener...

A baby who tried to take away everyone else's bottle at day-care will refuse his own at home.

## The Floor Fascination Factor

1.  If it's on your floor, it'll wind up in your baby's mouth.

2.  If it's in your baby's mouth, it'll wind up on your floor.

## The Junk Food Gourmet

Your baby probably will *not* get sick from eating:

1. Half an ice cream cone he found in the park.

2. Half a hot dog bun he found at the zoo.

3. A cigarette butt he found in the gutter.

4. A dead bug he found on your dining room floor.

5. A used piece of chewing gum he found under a restaurant table.

6. A few morsels of Rover's dry dog food.

If you watch him eat these yummies, *you* will get sick.

## Burping Precautions

Before burping your baby, take these precautions:

1. Open all the windows and doors to air the room.
2. Spread a drop cloth on the floor.
3. Don your bathing suit and a shower cap.
4. Run a bath.

## The "Right Time" To Wean

You've probably waited too long to wean your child if:

1. Your child is scheduled for his first appointment with the orthodontist.
2. Your child is accepted at an out-of-town college.
3. Your son's beard is fully grown.
4. Your son is no longer "carded" in bars.
5. Your daughter has missed a period.

# Baby Talk

## The Baby Talk Paradox

Instead of learning how to say "Mama" and "Dada," your one-year-old will succeed in teaching all older siblings and adults in the family how to babble in baby talk.

## Baby's First Word

Your baby's first word is that four-letter word you usually mutter when you discover that the diapers need changing, *again*.

## The Company Contingency

Your brilliant baby loves to say "Nite-Nite," wave "Bye-Bye," and blow kisses. Except when you have company.

# Babysitting

## Mom's "First Night on the Town" Worries

1. Will the baby cry all night?

2. Will the sitter forget to feed the baby?

3. Will the sitter forget to change the baby?

4. Will the sitter like the milk and cookies that were left for her?

5. Or will the sitter clean out the fridge?

## Dad's "First Night on the Town" Worries

1. Will he have enough change so Mom can call the sitter every half hour?

2. Will the sitter and her boyfriend have a better time in his bedroom than he does?

3. Will they drink all his beer, too?

## Dad's Child-Care Condition

Fathers are happy to babysit—as long as there's a football game on TV, beer in the fridge and the baby's asleep.

### Addendum

No matter how attentive Dad was, Mom can find five things he forgot to do which needlessly jeopardized the baby's life.

## The Weekend Forecast

The first time you are booked into a hotel for a relaxing weekend after having a baby:

1.  Your babysitter will cancel because she has a heavy date.

2.  Your baby will come down with the flu.

*Or,*

3.  You'll feel too guilty about leaving the baby to enjoy it.

# Travel

## The Airplane Axioms

1.  Baby will have a massive bowel movement moments before boarding.

2.  No matter how long the flight, your baby will not fall asleep until moments before landing.

### Diaper Bag Blues

No matter how much extra clothing, or how many diapers, bottles or toys you pack in a diaper bag, you won't have enough.

# The Second, Third (or More) Babies

## The Sure-Fire Conception Plan for Your Second Child

1. Tell your parents that you've decided to stop at one to do your part in solving the world population crisis.

2. Go even deeper into debt.

3. Buy an expensive two-bedroom house.

4. Sell all your baby furniture at a garage sale.

5. Buy a new post-pregnancy wardrobe.

6. Finally train your first child to sleep through the night.

## The Second Child Perspective

As soon as you've had your second child:

1. You appreciate the wisdom of those who have decided to stop at one.

2. You question the wisdom of those who have three or four.

3. You doubt the sanity of those with five or more.

## The Spacing Prescription

The optimum space between two babies is one generation.

## The Sanitary Solution

1.  When your first baby drops her pacifier, you sterilize it and wash the baby.

2.  When your second baby drops his pacifier, you pick it up off the floor, wipe it off on your shirt and pop it back in his mouth.

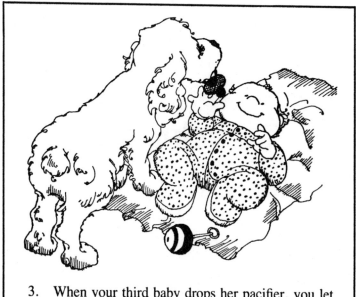

3.  When your third baby drops her pacifier, you let the dog fetch it for her.

## The Clothing Constant

1.  If your second child is the opposite sex of your first, you will have to buy a new set of baby clothes.

2.  If your second child is the same sex as your first, it will be born in a different season, so you'll still have to buy a new set of baby clothes.

## The Amnesia Effect—II

During labor with your first child, you will swear to yourself that you'll *never* put yourself through this agony again. Not until you are in labor with your second child will you remember why you made that vow.

## Mother Murphy's Law, Expanded

The more children you have, the more that can and will go wrong.

# Toddlers and Preschoolers

## The Knocking Nuisance

Your toddler has an uncanny knack for:

1. Knocking on your bedroom door when you are about to have sex.

2. Walking into your bedroom *without* knocking when you are already enjoying sex.

### Corollary

The more children you have, the less likely you are to enjoy sex undisturbed.

## The Kissing Contingency

1. A kiss will make most owies disappear.

2. Kissing owies is a full-time occupation.

## The "Company" Principle

Five minutes before the company arrives your toddler will:

1. Suddenly forget her potty training.

2. Suddenly forget her manners.

# Sleep

## The Nap Trap

1. The less your child naps, the more tired he gets.

2. The less your child naps, the more tired you get.

## The Price of Genius

1. The earlier you teach your children the ABCs, the sooner they'll be able to figure out those words you and your spouse have been spelling out, like b-e-d-t-i-m-e.

2. The sooner your children know how to tell time, the sooner they'll know exactly when to start their nightly bedtime delaying tactics.

## The Universal Lights-Out Routine

What every child says after you've said "Good night":

1. "I'm thirsty."

2. "I gotta go potty."

3. "Can I have another snuggle?"

4. "Can I have another story?"

5. "There's a monster under my bed."

### The Malice Moratorium

Never attribute to malice that which can be attributed to tiredness.

# The Terrible Twos

### The Valuable Variable

No matter how high you store your fragile heirlooms, your child will find a way to break them.

### The Childproofing Conundrum

The only individual in your household capable of opening the childproof aspirin bottle is your child.

### The Puddle Postulate

The larger and dirtier the puddle, the more likely your child is in it with new shoes.

#### Corollaries

1. Your child can't tell how deep a puddle is without stepping into it.

2. Your child *never* wears boots while performing this geological survey.

### Sure-Fire Trouble Starters

Your children suddenly begin fighting or crying...

1. When you pick up the phone.

2. When Daddy or Mommy comes home.

3. When the sermon begins in church.

4. When they pose for a photograph.

## The Quiet Conspiracy

1. The quieter it is in the bathroom, the more likely it is that your toddler is pouring the goldfish into the toilet bowl.

2. The quieter it is in the living room, the more likely it is that your toddler is finger-painting on the wall.

3. The quieter it is in the bedroom, the more likely it is that your toddler is pouring finger paints into the goldfish bowl and using the goldfish to paint the wall.

## The Case of the Broken Vase

It is easier to glue the vase together than to find the child who broke it.

## Missing Ingredients

1. The only things you can't find in the bathtub, amidst all the toys, boats and ducks, are soap and a washcloth.

2. What you *can* find are the contents of a full tube of toothpaste, half a can of shaving cream, and an entire roll of toilet paper.

## The Carpet Condition

The cleaner your carpet:

1. The more likely your toddler is to spill grape juice on it.

2. The more likely your toddler is to stomp on it in muddy boots.

3. The more likely your toilet-trained toddler is to make a "mistake" on it.

## The Case of the Clinging Vine

1. When you're on the phone, they're screaming in your ear.

2. When you're reading the newspaper, they're wrestling behind your chair.

3. When you're cooking in the kitchen, they're multiplying the mess.

4. When you're trying to leave for a night out, they're tugging on your leg.

5. When it's time to go to day-care, they're nowhere to be found.

# Mother Murphy's Guide to Shopping

In the supermarket your child will:

1.  Squeeze one Charmin and knock over the rest.

2.  Eat a few grapes and squish the rest.

3.  Eat a few cookies and crumble the rest.

4.  Mold the bread into little balls.

5.  Use a cucumber as a gun and "shoot" other shoppers.

6.  Climb out of the shopping cart and vanish the moment your head is turned.

7.  Wet through his diaper, down the shopping cart and onto the floor while you're waiting in the checkout line.

8.  Fall asleep as you start to carry your bags to the car.

# Discipline

## The Credibility Gap

1. Toddlers don't believe you mean it when you say "No."

2. They'll keep asking until you say "Yes."

3. If you don't say "Yes," they'll do what they wanted to anyway.

## The Forbidden Factor

The more firmly you forbid something, the more often it will be done.

## The Decibel Doctrine

1. The louder you yell, the less they hear you.

2. The less they hear you, the louder you must yell.

## The Striking Solution

When you catch your child hitting another child, grab him, spank him, and shout, "That will teach you to be violent!" It will.

## The Crying Conundrum

1. The less it hurts, the more they cry.

2. The more you comfort them, the more they cry.

## Positive Reinforcement Predicament

You can't "catch them doing something right" until they do something right.

## Tantrum Tactics

1. The intensity of the tantrum is inversely proportional to the precipitating event.

2. The more intense the tantrum, the less likely anyone can remember the precipitating event.

3. The more you insist that your two-year-old calm down, the longer the tantrum will last.

4. The more embarrassed you are by your child's tantrum, the longer it will last.

# Toilet Training

## Toilet Training Trauma

1. There are more than a thousand different toilet-training methods.

2. None of them work.

3. Don't worry...very few children wear diapers to kindergarten.

## The Toilet Training Trick

The day after you finally give up trying to train them, they'll go potty all by themselves.

## The Potty Prediction

1. As soon as toddlers are tightly bundled into snow suits, they will have to go potty.

2. If you take them to the bathroom before they go to bed, they will wet the bed.

3. If you forget to take them before they go to bed, they will wet the bed.

## The Bathroom Retreat

When you can't take it any longer, hide in the bathroom. That will buy you a few minutes of peace and quiet. Until they discover where you are and start pounding on the door.

## The Linen Law

The night after you change your toddler's bedsheets, he'll wet the bed.

## The Toilet Trap

1. Before you go shopping, they won't go to the bathroom.

2. As soon as you arrive at the store, they're dying to go to the bathroom.

3. Unfortunately, there is no toilet they can use in the store.

4. When you finally find a toilet they can use, it's too late.

# Reading

## The First Law of Literature

Your child's favorite book is the one you hate the most.

### Obverse

Your favorite children's book is the one your child ignores.

## The Reading Routine

1. When you want to read to them, they want to play.

2. They only want you to read to them when it's way past their bedtime.

3. No matter how many books you read to them at bedtime, it is never enough.

# Toys

## The Sharing Stalemate

1. Toddlers won't share their toys.

2. In fact, toddlers won't share anything that's theirs.

3. Toddlers want to share anything that belongs to someone else.

**Exception**
The only things toddlers share freely are germs.

## The Sharing Statute

The toy your toddler ignored for months will suddenly become his favorite the minute another child reaches for it.

## The Put-Away Ploy

1. It is much easier for your child to take the toys out than it is to put them away.

2. After playing with the toys, your child is "too tired" to put them away.

3. The child who is "too tired" to put any toys away will chase the ice cream truck around the block five minutes later.

## The Toy Ploy

The more expensive the toy, the more likely your child will only play with the box it came in.

## The Law of the Lost Toys

Any toys your child brings to a friend's house will be left there.

## The Disappearing Toy Phenomenon

The day after you've torn the house apart looking for your toddler's missing toy, you'll find it...in the toy box.

# Siblings

## The Mediation Mess

The fastest way to go crazy is to try to mediate a conflict between your children.

### Corollary

There is no lie detector or truth serum that can determine which of two toddlers hit the other first.

### Addendum

Two wrongs make a good fight.

## The Fairness Doctrine

1. Your children fight over what's fair.

2. Life isn't fair.

3. They fight nonstop.

## The Drink Dilemma

1.  If you don't pour drinks for two preschoolers perfectly equally, you'll have a fight on your hands.

2.  It is impossible to pour drinks for two preschoolers perfectly equally.

3.  No snack time is complete without the inevitable question, "How come he got more than me?"

# Eating

## The Law of the Diminishing Appetite

The longer it takes them to wash their hands, the greater the odds that they won't eat anything for dinner.

## The Hunger Factor

1. When they're at your supper table, they're not hungry.

2. When they're in your car, they're hungry.

## The Curiosity Factor

Your kids won't try anything new unless it is:

1. Deep-fried.

2. Smothered in ketchup.

3. Sprinkled with salt.

4. In a plastic fast-food container.

5. Dripping with frosting.

6. Sugar-coated.

7. Swimming in syrup.

## Nutrition Notes

1. If it's green, it's yukky.

2. If it's sugary, it's yummy.

3. If it's "good for you," forget it.

## The Dessert Distraction

1. The main reason kids eat lunch and supper is to get dessert.

2. The better the dessert, the more room they'll leave for it.

P.S. Don't bother trying to convince them that fruit is dessert.

# The Baker's Lament

The more they sample the frosting, the less they eat the cake.

### Addendum

The number of cookies that are actually baked is inversely proportional to the number of children "helping" you prepare them.

# The Cooking Consequence

1. You may be able to persuade your toddler to help you cook.

2. You won't be able to persuade your toddler to help you clean up the mess.

# The Clean Plate Syndrome

If you keep your child at the table until he eats all his vegetables, he will become sick to his stomach and keep you up all night changing his sheets.

# The Casserole Complaint

Children don't eat anything mixed together. Except fruit, nuts and syrup over ice cream.

# Successful Dieting Tip

Over half the food toddlers try to put into their mouths winds up instead on floors, seats, laps, bibs and faces. This prevents them from becoming overweight.

## The Cereal Criteria

Cereal won't be eaten unless it's sugared or colored, preferably both.

## Cookie Monster Maxims

1. The preferred way to eat a cookie is slowly, right in front of another sibling.

2. Cookies are also for crumbling all over the house. (After all, somebody's got to feed the bugs.)

3. Half-eaten cookies are buried in the crack between the sofa cushions.

## Fat Facts

1. Kids don't eat meat with fat on it. They are "allergic" to it.

I'M NOT GOING TO EAT THIS, THERE'S FAT ON IT!

2. Fat is a microscopic substance detected by children on pieces of meat they don't want to eat.

3. Kids are also "allergic" to all vegetables, inexpensive cuts of meat, and leftovers.

# Travel

## Traffic Trauma

If your children are in the car when you get a traffic ticket, they'll never forget it and you'll never live it down. (Never mind that it was their screaming in the back seat that caused you to miss the red light.)

## The Car Conversation

No car trip with a child is complete unless you hear these phrases:

1. "I gotta go potty!"
2. "I'm hungry."
3. "Are we there yet?"
4. "When will we be there?"
5. "He's on my side."
6. "She touched me."
7. "I'm gonna tell."

## The Beach Bonus

After spending a day at the beach with your child, you need a bulldozer to remove the sand from the back seat of your car.

# Schoolchildren

## The Law of Silence

Silence is rare. Some days, it's nonexistent.

## Leaving Logic

1. You can't wait for them to leave for camp.
2. The moment they're out of sight, you miss them.

## The Transportation Theorem

If your car has room for ''n'' kids, your child will want you to drive ''n + 1'' to the movies.

## The Puppy Love Principle

Your children will feed their new puppy dog. The day they get it home. And the days you threaten to take it back.

## The First Law of Electricity

The electric utility should put your kids on the payroll. For years they have been turning on all the lights in your home and forgetting to turn them off.

## The Slumber Secret

A slumber party is for:

1.  Gossiping, giggling and telling scary stories.
2.  Stuffing your face with popcorn, pizza and chocolate chip cookies.
3.  Calling boys.
4.  Dancing into the wee hours to impossibly loud rock music.

A slumber party is *not* for:

1.  Sleeping.
2.  Letting anyone else in the house sleep.

When everyone slumbers is the day *after* the party... *all* day.

## The Time Bind

1. The less time you give your children, the more time it takes to straighten up the mess.

2. No matter how much time you give them, they always want more.

## The Grocery Grumble

1. When you need help carrying the groceries into the house and putting them away, your kids are too busy watching TV.

2. By the time you've resolved the problem by turning off the TV and sending your kids to their rooms, the ice cream has melted all over the back seat and the meat has spoiled.

### Corollary

Your kids will run into the kitchen to ask what's to eat as soon as you've put all the groceries away.

# The Stay-at-Home Syndrome

The bigger your children's allowance, the less likely they are to run away from home.

## Delaying Tactics

The later you send them to bed, the longer they dawdle.

## The Snow Report

1. If Santa brings your child a brand new pair of skis, it'll be a "green" Christmas.

2. If Santa brings your child a new bicycle, there'll be four feet of snow on the ground until Easter.

# Tough Luck, Mom

## The Knock-Knock Nuisance

You have already heard every riddle and knock-knock joke your child will ever know. Several times.

## Mother Murphy's Rules of Medicine

The minute you announce you're sick:

1. The TV breaks.
2. Your husband says he's sicker and goes to bed.
3. Your daughter needs thirty treats to take to school.
4. There's no food in the house.

## Fan Etiquette

When attending your children's softball game:

1. Don't cheer too softly—they'll think you don't care.
2. Don't cheer moderately—your voice will get lost in the crowd.
3. Don't cheer too loudly—it will embarrass them.

## The Sanity Test

If you think you need psychotherapy during school vacations, wait until your kids are back in school and see if the symptoms persist.

## The Mother's Day Muddle

1. Your children serve you breakfast in bed on Mother's Day.

2. They also spill the coffee, burn the toast and wreck your kitchen.

3. You spend all afternoon cleaning up.

# Discipline

## The Golden Squawk

Say unto your children only that which you can stand them parroting back unto you.

# Newton's Law of Applied Parenting

All disciplinary actions trigger equally unpleasant reactions:

1. If you yell, you'll become hoarse.

2. If you spank, you'll hurt your hand.

3. If you ground your child, you'll have to stay home and play jailer.

4. In any case, you'll have an angry child on your hands.

# The Ultimate Child-Management Method

How to deal with objectionable behavior:

1. First, try reason.

2. Then, try ignoring it.

3. Then, try threats.

4. Then, try punishment.

5. Finally, when those techniques fail, say it's terrific and reward it.

### Corollary

The day you forget to nag your child about an objectionable behavior is the day it will disappear.

# The Consistency Exception

The easiest thing to be consistent about in childrearing is losing your temper.

# The Old Rope Trick

The more rope you give them, the more rope they'll ask for.

# The Law of Passive Resistance

The better it is for them, the more they refrain.
The fairer your decision, the more they complain.
The later it gets, the more they remain.
The more you need help, the more they abstain.

# The Law of Converse Behavior

1. The more tired you are, the more impossible they are.

2. The more you need quiet, the noisier they are.

3. The neater you are, the messier they are.

**Obverse**
The worse your mood, the worse their mood.

# The Rule of Respect

1. If you can't convince them, say it's a rule.

2. The rule that works is, "Because I said so."

# The Command Code

The only parental command your child will *not* disobey is
the command your child does not hear.

# The Mistake Maxim

You won't learn much from all the mistakes you made with
your first child because every child is completely different.
You'll make a completely new set of mistakes with each
one.

## The Monkey See, Monkey Do Doctrine

Children studiously model themselves after their parents. They copy every fault, vice and failure.

**Addendum**

If you want documented proof of your worst faults as a parent, listen to your kids playing with dolls.

# Siblings

### The Geography Factor

The closer you are when an injury occurs, the louder your child will cry.

### The Last Laugh Principle

He who laughs last gets hit first.

## The Quarrel Quotient

Two siblings' ability to keep a quarrel going is limited only by their need for sleep.

## The Blame Factor

1. When you separate two children who've been fighting, both will say, "He hit me first!"

2. The child who starts crying first is the one who is losing the fight.

3. The child who cries loudest is the one who started the fight.

## The Sibling Battlefield

Before you can settle a fight between two siblings, the seeds of a second fight have already been planted and have taken root.

## The Perfection Exceptions

Children are self-centered, impulsive, messy and loud. Apart from that they're perfect.

## The Presumption of Innocence

The more innocent your children look, the more guilty they really are.

# The Bathroom

## The Flushing Formula

1. Children *rarely* flush the toilet.

2. When you have company, children *never* flush the toilet.

## The Bathroom Riddle

1. Why does your child go to the bathroom before dinner? First clue: She doesn't wash her hands or use the toilet. Second clue: She goes in before the table is set, and comes out after the table is set.

2. Why does your child go to the bathroom after dinner? First clue: She doesn't wash her hands or use the toilet. Second clue: She goes in before the table is cleared, and comes out after the dishes are washed.

## The Hand-Washing Heresy

No matter how many times you have told your child to wash her hands before dinner, you will have to say it again. And she will point out that you haven't washed your hands either. Again.

## The "Me First" Fallacy

1. Everyone wants the first slice of cake.

2. Everyone wants the first can of soda pop.

3. Everyone wants to be first into the bathroom.

4. There's only one bathroom.

## The Washing Exception

The only time your child will voluntarily wash his face and hands is when he has finished off the chocolate layer cake you had baked for company, and wants to hide the "evidence."

### Addendum

The "evidence" will be on the bathroom towel.

# Television and Movies

## The Law of Energy Conservation

1. Your children can't hear you say, "It's time to turn off the TV," because it's on too loud.

2. The only way to get the attention of children watching TV is to turn it off.

## The Boredom Solution

1. The more toys they have, the more bored they are.

2. The more bored they are, the more likely they are to watch TV.

3. The more TV channels you receive, the less likely they are to do anything besides watch TV.

4. The more TV they watch, the more toys they will see advertised that they want you to buy them (which they won't play with because they're too busy watching TV).

## The Movie Deadlock

1. The only movies you'll let them see are rated "G" or "PG."

2. The only movies they want to see are rated "R."

## The Must-See Movie Maxim

The more you hate a movie your kids have seen on TV, the more intensely they want to see it again. And again. And again.

## The Saturday Morning Forecast

On Saturday morning:

1. If it's raining outside, your child will want to stay inside and watch TV.

2. If it's too hot outside, your child will want to stay inside and watch TV.

3. If it's too cold outside, your child will want to stay inside and watch TV.

4. If it's a perfect day, your child will want to stay inside and watch TV.

# Toys

## The "Thank You" Farce

By the time they get around to writing a thank-you note for the gift, it's already broken.

## The Breakdown Guarantee

1. If it's breakable, your kids will break it.

2. If it's "unbreakable," your kids will break it.

3. When it's broken, they'll expect *you* to fix it.

## The Truth About Toys

The more expensive the toy, the more likely it is to be broken or ignored five minutes after it is removed from its box.

### Corollary

Your children's favorite toys belong to their friends.

## The "Everything Is Greener" Syndrome

1. Their friends' toys are always better than their toys.

2. Their friends' TV is always better than their TV.

3. Their friends' house is always nicer than their house.

4. Their friends' parents are always nicer than their parents.

5. Unfortunately, their friends' parents don't want extra lodgers.

# Doctors and Medicine

## The Career Choice

1. If you don't let your son play doctor, he'll grow up to be a gynecologist.

2. The boy who plays doctor with all the girls in your neighborhood will grow up to be a priest.

## The Posture Discovery

Bad posture *isn't* caused by slouching. Bad posture *is* caused by:

1. Reading books.
2. Studying for tests.
3. Doing science projects for extra credit.
4. Practicing the violin.
5. Eating vegetables.

## The Appointment Aggravation

By the time you get a doctor's appointment for your sick child, he's back in school setting a new record for sit-ups.

## The Apple Admonition

1. An apple a day keeps the doctor away.
2. You can't get your child to eat an apple a month, let alone an apple a day.
3. That's why there are more than 24,000 affluent pediatricians in North America today.

## The Weather-Health Connection

1. If it's damp, your child catches a cold.
2. If it's chilly, your child catches the flu.
3. If it's hot, your child gets dehydrated.
4. If it's perfect, your child plays outside and catches poison ivy.

## Medical Magic

A spoonful of sugar helps the medicine go down. That makes both the doctor *and* the dentist rich.

## The Chocolate Conspiracy

Relatives who bring chocolates when they visit don't pay your dental bills.

# Eating

## Unbelievable, but True

The child who loves carrots wears bifocal glasses.
The child who loves sardines is flunking third-grade math.
The child who eats only junk food is the class athlete.
The child who swims right after eating wins the race.

## The Nutrition Test

1. The longer you take preparing a meal, the longer it remains uneaten.

2. The more nutritious the meal, the more energetically your kids shout, "Yuk!"

## The Last Straw

Straws aren't for drinking. Straws are for:

1. Holding liquid (by sipping and then putting a finger over the opening).

2. Blowing bubbles in a drink.

3. Blowing the paper wrapper in someone's eye.

# Food Warnings

1. Kids don't eat Oreo cookies. Just the white stuff inside.

2. Kids don't eat peas. They mash them.

3. Kids don't eat mashed potatoes. They irrigate them with gravy.

4. Kids don't eat crusts. They leave them for the birds.

5. Kids don't eat spinach. They compact it.

6. Kids don't eat broccoli. They decapitate it.

7. Kids don't eat spaghetti. They suck the sauce off it.

8. Kids don't eat milk shakes. They blow bubbles in them.

9. Kids don't eat a double ice cream cone. The top scoop falls off and the bottom scoop drips out.

10. Kids don't chew gum. They swallow it (accidentally).

# Eating Exceptions

1. The only vegetable your child eats cheerfully is jelly beans.

2. The only seafood your child eats cheerfully is salt-water taffy.

3. The only green thing your child eats cheerfully is mint chocolate chip ice cream.

4. The only time your child does *not* reach for a soft drink container in the refrigerator (instead of milk or juice) is when it's the empty one she put back in the refrigerator.

# The Dinnertime Dilemma

1. Your child never has to go potty before dinner.

2. Your child always has to go potty after everyone is seated at the table and has started eating.

3. Once your child leaves the table to go potty, you won't see her again—until it's time for dessert.

## The Dinner Paradox

The less your children eat at dinner, the more likely they are to ask for seconds on dessert.

### Addendum

A child's appetite for dessert is virtually unlimited.

## The Starving Children Syndrome

After magnanimously contemplating the starving multitudes in every Third World country whose name you can remember, your child still will not try spinach, broccoli or cauliflower.

# School

## The Law of First-Day Trauma

Your child's first day at school will be a tearful occasion. For you.

## The First Law of Geometry

The shortest distance between two kids in homeroom is measured by the flight of a spitball.

## The Law of Selective Recall

1. Don't expect your grade-schoolers to tell you what happened at school. They won't.

2. Don't be surprised if they tell you *everything* that happened on their favorite TV show.

## The Last-Minute Demand

Five minutes before the school bus is scheduled to arrive, your child will tell you that he's expected to bring six dozen homemade cookies to his class party.

## Quick Recovery Recipe

Your sick child will feel a lot better as soon as the school bus leaves your stop.

## The Smartness Quotient

The smarter your children are in school, the smarter their mouths are at home.

## The Early-To-Rise Rule

The later you stayed out on Sunday night, the earlier your child will have to be at school on Monday for a special band rehearsal.

# Dressing

## The Bargain Bonanza

The best sales on children's clothes are advertised the day after you've purchased your child's entire school wardrobe.

## Weather Predictions

When it snows: your child won't wear a hat.

When it rains: your child won't wear boots.
When it's cold: your child won't wear an undershirt.
No matter what the weather: your child won't wear what you want her to wear.

## Clothes Consciousness

The more expensive the jacket your child wears to school, the more likely your child will:

1. Rip the pocket during recess.

2. Leave an indelible ink marker in the pocket all day— with the cap off.

3. Loan it to a friend.

4. Lose it.

# Communication

## Mother Murphy's Rejoinder to P. T. Barnum

1.  Your child can be fooled only once.

2.  Your child can be bribed many times.

## How To Improve Family Communications

The best way to open up lines of communication with all your children is to go to bed early with your spouse, turn on some romantic music and lock the bedroom door. Your entire family will soon be camped outside your bedroom door with urgent matters to discuss in depth.

## The Facts of Life

It's a waste of time to tell your children the facts of life. They already know them. Besides, they've already taught them to the kids next door.

## The Hospitality Hangup

When your kids have friends over, never invite them to "make themselves at home," or they'll turn it into a zoo.

## Six-Year-Old Skepticism

Your six-year-old doesn't believe in Santa Claus, the Tooth Fairy or the story that you and your spouse are "taking a nap" at ten o'clock on Saturday morning.

## Excusemanship

Children have brilliant excuses for everything:

1. If they're late: "My nose was running and I had to chase it."

2. If they can't sit still at the dinner table: "Wiggling is good for my digestion."

3. If their rooms are a mess: "I tried putting everything away neatly once, and couldn't find anything."

4. If they're biting their nails: "I eat only organic foods...and prefer snacks that are handy."

# Names

## The Name Game

The more children you have, the more names you will call before you hit on the name of the child you are calling to the telephone.

## The Sticks and Stones Surprise

Sticks and stones *won't* break their bones, but names *will always* hurt them.

### Corollary

No matter how innocuous you think your child's name is, he'll be teased about it.

# Teenagers

## The Parent Effectiveness Delusion

When you finally think you've got child-rearing under control, your child becomes a teenager. And you're back behind the eight ball.

## Rule of the Rising Rates

The more responsibility you delegate to your teenager, the more your insurance rates increase.

## The Clean Machine

The only help in cleaning you can count on from your teenager is that your refrigerator will be cleaned out within half an hour after you return from the grocery store.

## The Sound's Effect

The bad news: Your teenage son is proud of his ability to belch loud enough to wake the entire neighborhood.
The worse news: He's trying to increase his range.

## Tornado Warning

Your teenager's room resembles the aftermath of a tornado. *After* it's been cleaned.

## The Crush Condition

1.  The guy she has a crush on doesn't know she's alive.

2.  The more she gets to know him, the less she likes him.

## The Law of Irrationality

Teenagers don't act rationally, even when all other possibilities have been exhausted.

80

## Selective Recall Rule

Teenagers remember (and repeat) your foulest epithets, but forget their promises to wash the dishes.

## The Pocket-Money Maxims

1. If your teenager has a job, he'll have more spending money than you do.

2. If you need to borrow a buck, "it'll cost you."

# The Generation Gap

## Sure-Fire Teenager Torture

Whatever you wear or say in public will embarrass your teenager.

### Warning

Don't laugh, sing or dance.

### Double Warning

For best results, don't breathe.

### Corollary

Your teenager will walk in front of you or behind you—anywhere but near you.

## The Rejection Response

When you are rejected by your teenagers, don't be discouraged. It only lasts for about seven years.

## The Compliment Caveat

1.  The teenager who says, "You're a great Mom" is about to ask to borrow your car.

2.  The teenager who says, "You're the best Mom in the whole wide world" is about to ask to borrow your car plus $25 for gas and expenses.

3.  The teenager who says, "You're the best Mom in the universe" has just totaled your car.

## The Fogey Factor

1.  When kids are young, they think their parents are the "smartest people in the world."

2.  When they become teenagers, they think their parents are "hopelessly old-fashioned and have forgotten everything they ever knew."

# Discipline

## Dangerous Threat

Don't say, "Just wait till you have children of your own." You might not have to wait very long.

## The Futility of Spanking

You need to come up with an alternative to spanking when your child is (suddenly) bigger than you are.

# Doctors and Medicine

## The Dental Dilemma

The best time to schedule dental appointments for your teen-agers is during their toughest class. Otherwise, they won't go.

## The Acne Discovery

Acne *isn't* caused by eating chocolate. Acne *is* caused by:

1. Making the bed.
2. Washing before meals.
3. Flushing the toilet.
4. Closing the refrigerator door.
5. Washing the dishes.
6. Taking out the garbage.
7. Turning off the lights.

## The Revenge of the Tooth Fairy

When you visit your teenager's orthodontist, remember to admire his new car. You paid for it.

# School

## The Put-Down Reflex

1. Anyone who gets better grades than your teenager is a "nerd."

2. Anyone who is more popular than your teenager is an "airhead."

## The Quiet Quandary

1. The noisier it is in your teenager's bedroom, the more likely he is to be studying for finals.

2. The quieter it is in your teenager's bedroom, the more likely he is to be studying your sex manuals.

## Lateness Logic

Teenagers spend more time making up excuses for not getting their term papers in on time than it would have taken to write them.

## The Driver's License

Just because he's on the track team don't expect him to walk, run or bike a half-mile to school after he gets his driver's license.

## The Popularity Predicament

1. Teenagers believe they won't be popular unless they have expensive clothes and a fast car.

2. If they take an after-school job, they can afford expensive clothes and a fast car.

3. Between schoolwork and their job, there's no time to reap the rewards of popularity.

## The Dirty Dish Dilemma

If your teenager breaks down and washes the dishes, don't complain that the dishes are still dirty. Unless you don't want her to ever wash the dishes again. Which might not be such a bad idea. (And that's exactly what she wants you to conclude.)

### Corollary

If she volunteers to do the dishes, she has two finals the next day that she should be studying for.

# Manners

## The Manners Maxims

1. Your child will flush the toilet and close the refrigerator door the day he moves out of the house. (His roommates will kill him if he doesn't.)

2. Your child will excuse himself after burping the day he tries to teach his own child good manners.

### The Manners Mess

1. Their dates don't notice their atrocious manners.

2. Their dates' manners are equally atrocious.

# Dressing

### The Budget Breaker

Teenagers can spend more money on a single outfit than you'll spend on your entire wardrobe in a year.

### The Dictates of Fashion

If it fits but it's not in fashion—they won't wear it.
If it fits and is in fashion but isn't brand new—they won't wear it, either.

#### Corollary

When you buy your teenager a gift of clothing, the most likely response you'll get is, "Only a nerd would wear that!"

### The Clothing Condition

The more you detest your daughter's latest outfit, the more often she wears it.

# Telephone

### Ma Bell's Law

1. When the phone rings, it's for your teenager.

2. When the phone bill arrives, it's for you.

### The Sulking Exception

Teenagers sulk. Except when they're on the phone.

### Selective Hearing Rule

1. When they think the call's for you, they can't hear the phone ring even if they're standing right next to it.

2. When they're expecting a call from their friends, they can hear the phone ring from the shower.

**Corollary**

Teenagers will only take messages from aluminum siding salesmen or fund raisers.

# Communication

### The Dialog Dilemma

1. When you want to talk to your teenagers, they're too busy.

2. When your teenagers want to talk to you, you're rushing out the door, late for work.

3. What they want to talk about is what you have to buy for them on your way home from work.

**Corollary**

Your teenagers also are quite willing to discuss their innermost thoughts when you're:

1. Taking a bath or otherwise occupied in the bathroom.

2. Talking on the telephone.

3. Trying to fill out your tax returns.

4. Sound asleep.

## The Communication Breakdown

1. When you ask a question, they don't respond.

2. When you give them an answer, they talk back.

## The Communication Gap

## Related Oddity

1. Teenagers become talkative when they're in the bathroom.

2. You can't hear a word they're saying because the door is closed and the faucet is running.

# Send us your "laws"!

Mother Murphy is now collecting "laws" for another book. Her next book will cover a broad range of topics including dating, love and romance, sex, marriage and divorce, cooking, cleaning, home decoration and repair, gardening, crafts, hobbies, working, shopping, fashion, health, diet, fitness, sports, money, aging, relatives and family matters, philosophy, psychology, fads, weather...you name it.

**Submission rules:** Each person submitting a "law" shall provide his/her full name and address. The first person to submit a "law" will receive credit in the book plus a free copy when it is published, if selected (unless otherwise requested below). All "laws" submitted must have their original source designated (individual, magazine, newspaper, book or other) unless completely original. All "laws" submitted are assigned to and become the property of Meadowbrook, Inc., for publication and all other purposes. "Laws" submitted are subject to editing before publication. "Laws" to be published will be selected by Mother Murphy and "laws" not used will not be returned.

I have read and understood and agree to abide by all the above rules.

Signature_____

(Please print or type)

Name_____

Address_____

City, State & Zip_____

☐ I *do not* want my name published with my submission

**Write your "law" on the lines below.**

_____

_____

_____

Source, if not completely original

**Please send all submissions to:** Mother Murphy, Meadowbrook Creations, 18318 Minnetonka Blvd., Deephaven, MN 55391

## David, We're Pregnant!
*by Lynn Johnston*
101 laughing-out-loud cartoons about the humorous side of having a baby by the creator of the "For Better or For Worse" comic strip.

**Order #1049**

## Hi Mom! Hi Dad!
*by Lynn Johnston*
101 cartoons about the funny things that happen to new parents.

**Order #1139**

## Do They Ever Grow Up?
*by Lynn Johnston*
A hilarious, 101-cartoon survival guide for parents of the tantrum and tears set.

**Order #1089**

## Discipline Without Shouting or Spanking
*by Jerry Wyckoff, Ph.D., and Barbara C. Unell*
This useful book functions like a first aid book for misbehavior. It contains solutions to the most common preschool behavior problems.

**Order #1079**

# Order Form

| Qty | Title | Author | Order No. | Unit Cost | Total |
|-----|-------|--------|-----------|-----------|-------|
| | Dads Say The Dumbest Things | Lansky/Jones | 4220 | $5.95 | |
| | David, We're Pregnant! | Johnston, L. | 1049 | $5.95 | |
| | Discipline Without Shouting or Spanking | Wyckoff/Unell | 1079 | $5.95 | |
| | Don't Call Mommy | McBride, M. | 4039 | $4.95 | |
| | Do They Ever Grow Up? | Johnston, L. | 1089 | $5.95 | |
| | Empty Nest Symphony | McBride, M. | 4080 | $4.95 | |
| | Grandma Knows Best | McBride, M. | 4009 | $4.95 | |
| | Hi Mom! Hi Dad! | Johnston, L. | 1139 | $5.95 | |
| | How To Be A Catholic Mother | Dodds, B. | 4230 | $4.95 | |
| | Mother Murphy's Law, | Lansky, B. | 1149 | $3.95 | |
| | Mother Murphy's 2nd Law | Lansky, B. | 4010 | $4.95 | |
| | Over the Hill Survival Guide | Feigel/Walker | 4210 | $5.95 | |
| | Parents' Guide To Dirty Tricks | Dodds, B. | 4190 | $4.95 | |
| | | | | Subtotal | |
| | | | | Shipping and Handling (see below) | |
| | **Meadowbrook Press** | | | MN residents add 6% sales tax | |
| | | | | Total | |

YES, please send me the books indicated above. Add $1.25 shipping and handling for the first book and $.50 for each additional book. Add $2.00 to total for books shipped to Canada. Overseas postage will be billed. Allow up to 4 weeks for delivery. Send check or money order payable to Meadowbrook Press. No cash or C.O.D.'s please. Quantity discounts available upon request. Prices subject to change without notice.

## Send book(s) to:

Name_____

Address_____

City_____ State_____ Zip_____

☐ Check enclosed for $_____, payable to Meadowbrook Press

☐ Charge to my credit card (for purchases of $10.00 or more only)

☐ Phone Orders call: (800) 338-2232 (for purchases of $10.00 or more only)

Account #_____  ☐ Visa ☐ MasterCard

Signature_____  Exp. date_____

Meadowbrook Press, 18318 Minnetonka Boulevard, Deephaven, MN 55391
(612) 473-5400
Toll free (800) 338-2232